THE BELIEVERS' GUIDE TO FIGHTING DEPRESSION

Revelation from Elijah's Time in the Cave

A 7-Day Devotional for Those Battling Depression

Jamal Ross

Copyright © 2022 by **Jamal Ross**

All rights reserved. No part of this publication may be reproduced, distributed, or transmitted in any form or by any means, without prior written permission.

Unless otherwise noted, Scripture quotations are taken from the New King James Version®. Copyright © 1982 by Thomas Nelson, Inc. Used by permission. All rights reserved.

Scripture quotations marked (ESV) are taken from The ESV® Bible (The Holy Bible, English Standard Version®) copyright © 2001 by Crossway, a publishing ministry of Good News Publishers. ESV® Text Edition: 2011. The ESV® text has been reproduced in cooperation with and by permission of Good News Publishers. Unauthorized reproduction of this publication is prohibited. Used by permission. All rights reserved.

Scripture quotations marked (NLT) are taken from the Holy Bible, New Living Translation, copyright © 1996, 2004, 2015 by Tyndale House Foundation. Used by permission of Tyndale House Publishers, Inc., Carol Stream, Illinois 60188. All rights reserved.

Renown Publishing
www.renownpublishing.com

The Believers' Guide to Fighting Depression / Jamal Ross
ISBN-13: 978-1-952602-95-5

Contents

Who Is Elijah? III

The Threat: Perception Is Not Reality XI

Depressed Mood: Running into Isolation 1

Reject Thoughts of Death: Overcome and Live 13

Loss of Appetite: Arise and Eat 27

Disturbances of Sleep and Concentration: Awake and Move 39

Tiredness, Fatigue, and Psychomotor Changes: Go in Strength 51

Worthlessness and Guilt: What Are You Doing Here? 61

Still, Small Voice: Your New Life Awaits 71

About the Author 83

About Renown Publishing 85

Notes 87

PREFACE

Who Is Elijah?

Elijah was a prophet in Israel who performed several miracles in his day. One of his best-known miracles involved ending a three-year drought in Israel. The story of Elijah and the miracle of the rain provides us a glimpse into the symptoms of depression and how we can find ourselves in a place of discouragement and isolation despite our accomplishments.

Initially, in response to the disobedience of Israel, Elijah stated, "There shall not be dew nor rain these years, except at my word" (1 Kings 17:1b). In other words, Elijah called for a drought. In the industrial world of today, the significance of a drought in an agricultural society can be lost on us. In those days, the lack of rain translated to a lack of crops, resulting in poverty and the death of livestock and families. With drought came great suffering. Therefore, an end to a drought meant an end to misery; it represented a brighter tomorrow. Elijah also helped bring about an end to this drought, but prayer, obedience, and faith were required on his part.

To better acquaint ourselves with the miracle of the rain and the disobedience of Israel and their king, we require some historical context. After the reign of King Solomon, the kingdom of David had split into northern and southern realms. The Southern Kingdom comprised the tribes of Judah, Benjamin, and Levi. Rehoboam was the son of Solomon and the king of the Southern Kingdom. The Northern Kingdom comprised the remaining tribes of Israel. Jeroboam was the first ruler of the Northern Kingdom, which God had promised him.

Jeroboam become concerned that the people in the Northern Kingdom would visit Jerusalem, to the south, to offer sacrifices to God, and afterward their loyalties would turn to Rehoboam. Instead of believing in the promises of God, therefore, Jeroboam created two golden calves and instructed the children of Israel to worship these sculptures, not God. In this way, Jeroboam believed the people in the Northern Kingdom would not need to return to Jerusalem to worship (1 Kings 12:28–33). And so, the sin of idol worship grew out of the king's manipulation and his lack of belief in God's promise. The actions of Jeroboam had a ripple effect on later kings of the Northern Kingdom.

Fast forward to the reign of Ahab in the North: this disobedience was alive and worse than ever (1 Kings 16:30). The reign of Ahab was particularly troubling, as he continued to foster idol worship of varying kinds. Ahab entered an arranged marriage to Jezebel (1 Kings 16:31) as a strategic alliance between the Northern Kingdom of Israel and the Phoenicians, who were an important seafaring and merchant people in the Mediterranean. With this alliance, the Northern Kingdom fell further away from God, because Jezebel brought many priests and prophets of Baal, an idol of the Phoenician people of Canaan, into the land of Israel. The people of Israel strayed from the love of God and instead worshiped Baal.

Elijah, whose name meant, "Yahweh is my God,"[1] was the prophet of his day. True to his name, Elijah took a stand against idol worship and became determined to prove the only God was Yahweh. As a result, he called a three-year drought in Israel. This drought had great significance because Baal represented the god of rain and thunder for the people of Canaan. The drought was used to show the people of Israel that God alone was their provider, who would eventually bring the rain once more.

When Elijah finally called an end to the drought, he did it in dramatic fashion. Prior to this miracle, Ahab sent representatives from kingdom to kingdom to search for Elijah. Now, Jezebel had killed many prophets of the Lord, so Elijah's life was in great danger. Nonetheless, at the word of God, Elijah presented himself to Ahab with boldness and commanded a challenge (1 Kings 18:22–24).

Elijah ordered Ahab to gather all the people of Israel to Mount Carmel, where he confronted the 450 prophets of Baal and 400 prophets of Asherah with a test. Elijah would build an altar and offer a sacrifice, and the prophets of the false gods Baal and Asherah would do the same. The true God would answer from heaven with fire. Elijah continued in his boldness and challenged the people of Israel to make a decision to serve the Lord that day.

Elijah worked alone to prepare his own sacrifice. He dug a trench around it and used a lot of water, which was in scarce supply, to pour upon the sacrifice. The water flowed into the trenches. Elijah prayed, and God answered with fire, consuming everything upon the altar, including the sacrifice and the water in the trenches (1 Kings 18:38). At this, the Israelites' heart turned back to God, and they killed the prophets of Baal and Asherah. Hope was in the air, but the rain hadn't come yet.

> *The drought ended and fulfilled the promise of God.*

Elijah had more work to do before the rain fell. He went to the top of Mount Carmel, put his head between his knees so he could not see his surroundings, and prayed. Afterward, he sent his servant to look at the sky for a sign of rain. Elijah accepted nothing less than the promise from God: he sent his servant back seven times, until a cloud the size of a man's hand appeared (1 Kings 18:44).

At this slight change, Elijah announced the coming of a torrential rain. He told Ahab to get something to eat and drink and to prepare his chariot before the rain arrived. Then, God gave Elijah tremendous strength to outrun the king's chariot for twenty miles as they raced back to the city of Jezreel. The rain came, ending the drought and fulfilling the promise of God.

In the midst of the miracle, Elijah received a threat from Jezebel. Instead of praising God or celebrating the rain, Jezebel threatened to kill Elijah after hearing what had happened to the prophets of Baal and Asherah. Elijah became discouraged. With a sense of fear and impulsivity, Elijah ran, leaving his servant behind and traveling through wilderness into a cave of depression (1 Kings 19:1–4).

Though God was still with Elijah, his perception of his situation had changed. The threat of Jezebel never came to pass, but fear and discouragement had taken root in Elijah's heart. He had replaced his boldness and faith with depression. Leaving the miracle of the rain behind, he ran from his responsibilities as a prophet.

Like Elijah, those dealing with depression can be gifted, talented, and effective. Depression can be far-reaching and affect those who are charismatic and influential. We can be the "life of the party" yet suffer from depression. But do not let depression overshadow your gifts; instead, learn the weapons of God to help recognize and defeat this condition. God has given you, like Elijah, strength to accomplish feats that seem impossible.

When you struggle with depression, you may ask several questions such as, "God, my heart is pure and turned in Your direction, so why do I feel like this? Why have so many threats and difficulties come my way?" We will answer these questions, and more, during our week in devotion to Jesus.

Remember, in life we will have trials, but Jesus has overcome them all (John 16:33). Our trust is in Him. God has given you strength, joy, and a future filled with happiness as our reassurance that depression does not belong in your midst. With the help of God, you will conquer depression and walk into a life filled will great joy that overflows from your heart.

"Then Jezebel sent a messenger to Elijah, saying, "So let the gods do to me, and more also, if I do not make your life as the life of one of them by tomorrow about this time."

1 KINGS 19:2

INTRODUCTION

The Threat: Perception Is Not Reality

Life's troubles have found you. Some event or threat has thrown you into the realm of depression. You may have been mired in this state for only a few days or for weeks, even months. Formerly familiar surroundings and circumstances now seem strange and incomprehensible. You feel as though you are a shadow of your former self. You carry out your routines in an automated way, passively completing tasks and being cordial to others. Your smile conceals a broken heart and a soul that longs for better days. Even when your laughter is genuine, painful thoughts lurk in the recesses of your mind.

Maybe the possibility of losing your job and suffering financial collapse knocks at your door. Perhaps a broken marriage or separation with the threat of divorce has entered your life. Or you lay down to sleep at night with insecurity about singleness and the specter of a life lived alone. Anxiety about a seriously ill loved one may awaken you in the morning. Dark memories of an abusive childhood may stalk you throughout the day. A spiral of negative thoughts and possibilities takes over your imagination.

Your difficulties are real, but the threats consuming your mind are not. After the drought in Israel broke, Jezebel had every intention of killing Elijah, but this did not occur. The threats occupying your mind may seem immediate and real. They may have come to pass before, whether in your life or someone else's. Yet, these threats will not come near you now, because God is in control and your perception of this difficult moment is not reality. As God protected Elijah with a promise, He has an amazing promise for your life. Therefore, let your heart be filled with encouragement and joy! Jesus is the shield around you and the lifter of your head (Psalm 3:3). Because of Him, better days are on your horizon.

That said, make no mistake—depression is a formidable opponent that has far-reaching effects. One in five adults will suffer with depression during their lifetime.[2] Doctors recognize depression in about half of people who seek assessment.[3] Many kinds of life events can lead to depression. Those who are divorced, separated, or widowed have the highest rates of depression.[4] Children of divorced parents have an increased risk of developing depression.[5] Depression can be a generation curse as well: children of parents who suffer from depression have a higher chance of developing depression themselves.[6][7] Alcohol, drugs, and co-dependent relationships can provide temporary relieve, only to fuel the fire of depression in the days to come.

The *Diagnostic and Statistical Manual of Mental Disorders* (DSM-5) is a book used by health care professionals to diagnose mental health conditions, including depression.[8] According to the DSM-5, those with major depressive disorder have a depressed mood, such as feelings of sadness, emptiness, or hopelessness. Also, those with major depressive disorder can have anhedonia, which involves lack of interest and pleasure in most, if not all, activities of life. With anhedonia, you may not enjoy gardening, a daily walk, or spending time with your family.

Importantly, you can feel depression without being depressed. Feelings of depression do not necessarily mean you suffer from major depressive disorder, which is only diagnosed when it predominates your mood greater than fifty percent of the time and persists for no less than two weeks. In essence, we all can feel "down in the dumps" from time to time, but major depression occurs when feelings of emptiness, sadness, and depression fill our thoughts, impact our daily life, and last for a prolonged time.

Other symptoms of depression include changes to eating habits, weight, sleep, and energy level. You may find yourself not eating enough or eating too much. As a result, you may lose or gain drastic amounts of weight. If you suffer depression, you may sleep too much, or not enough, and feel fatigued, without energy. There can also be difficulties with concentration, where you find it hard to focus on simple tasks such as reading.

With extreme symptoms of depression, you may have thoughts of harming yourself or others.[9][10] Remember, these thoughts are not of God, and you should reject them immediately!

Depression comes in various shades; with more severe forms of this disease, a physiological basis can be the culprit. Medication and counseling can be effective means to treat depression, but they are not enough, because you need the power and promises of God to defeat this illness. You need to know the promises of God so you can have the hope that leaves depression behind. When you leave the counselor's office, you need the Holy Spirit to walk with you, provide comfort, and guide your decisions. Do not make the terrible mistake of believing you don't need the power of God to fight depression! In all things, you are more than conquerors through Christ Jesus (Romans 8:37).

> *If we inspect your life, there are bright moments filled with great promise.*

If you inspect your life, you will find bright moments filled with great promise. These bright points become more brilliant with each day you walk with God. He cancels every threat, replacing it with a promise.

If you have experienced financial ruin, you will have great abundance. Instead of being a borrower, you will be a lender to many (Deuteronomy 28:12).

If your marriage is on the brink of divorce, God will restore the covenant with your spouse and resurrect your marriage from the dead. If you are single, God will reveal your spouse, who will have the heart of God, to you. If you have lost a loved one, God will bring peace to your life as you make new friends and restore old relationships.

If you have suffered physical, sexual, or emotional abuse as a child or adult, God will ease those painful memories by connecting you to people who value and cherish you. You will receive "two blessings for each of your troubles" (Zechariah 9:12 NLT). Your joyful moments will overcome all the memories of your past (see Genesis 41:51).

In the end, God's enemies did not kill Elijah; ultimately, Jezebel suffered the very fate with which she had threatened the prophet (2 Kings 9:30–37). Elijah continued to perform miracles and complete the work of God. Likewise, the looming threats and negative thoughts that come against you will not become your reality. They are trying to prevent you from completing the work of God, so you must reject them. Instead, give your anxieties to God, because He cares for you (1 Peter 5:7). Reject every negative emotion, instead finding your joy in Jesus, and "He shall give you the desires of your heart" (Psalm 37:4). You cannot imagine the life God has in store for you (1 Corinthians 2:9). Keep living, hoping, and believing for a better tomorrow.

You have an amazing life to live and a God-given purpose to fulfill. The emotional suffering you are experiencing cannot compared to the joy God has in store for you (Romans 8:18). God loves and wants the best for you. Any thought that says otherwise is a lie. Cast these lies behind you and live a God-driven, purpose-filled life.

During each day of this devotional, we will learn more about symptoms of depression and how to use the word of God to attack every symptom of this condition. Each day also contains a song to help bring you close to God and strengthen you in worship.

Be encouraged! Resist the temptation to view your life through the lens of emotions that stem from your troubles, and view your life from the perspective of God's promises. Your hope will not disappoint (Romans 5:5). Jesus will bring you out of the darkness and break your chains into pieces (Psalm 107:14). Nothing will hold you from the laughter and joy of your future. When Jesus sets you free, you are truly free (John 8:36). You will live in peace beyond understanding (Philippians 4:7), and you will continue to live a blessed life as you conquer depression with prayer and faith. God has carried you this far—He won't stop now!

Song of the Day:
"Won't Stop Now"
by Elevation Worship.[11]

Resources

National Institute of Mental Health

Do you want to find out more about depression? The National Institute of Health has an excellent website that covers different types of depression, such as major depression, seasonal affective disorder, and depression related to pregnancy. The site also covers different treatment options for depression. This is a great place to start if you would like to know about depression and how it affects all ages groups.

You can find more information at:
https://www.nimh.nih.gov/health/publications/depression.

"And when he saw that, he arose and ran for his life, and went to Beersheba, which belongs to Judah, and left his servant there."

1 KINGS 19:3

DAY ONE

Depressed Mood: Running into Isolation

The drought was over. God had fulfilled His promise, and rain quenched the parched earth. The people of Israel had turned their hearts to God. Joy was in the air, but a threat from Jezebel reached Elijah. With this threat, memories of the miracle of rain seemed to fade. Jezebel's threat had uprooted their joy and planted seeds of fear and discouragement in their hearts.

Though Elijah had waited patiently for his prayer to be answered on top of Mount Carmel before the rain came, he now formulated an impulsive decision, in the absence of prayer: he would run away from his obligation. Elijah escaped to the land of Judah, the tribe of praise. Ironically, instead of praising and seeking the Lord for direction, Elijah isolated himself, leaving his servant in Beersheba. He sat alone as depression festered.

There can be a myriad of difficult moments in life that cause us to make impulsive decisions, isolate ourselves, and run from responsibility. A pending divorce, problems at work, a child who has left home, or an illness can bring us to an intersection in our choices where we desire an escape rather than confrontation or commitment to our responsibilities. It is not necessarily one event that causes us to run from our obligations, but a series of trials that pummel our souls. At times, our troubles seem unrelenting.

As an impulse, we decide to accept a divorce, quit a job, declare we will never again speak to our children, or accept that an illness will lead to death. We do not make these decisions in faith, but in fear and discouragement. Instead of devising our plans of escape in prayer, we attempt to use our rational mind that leans on our own wisdom. We isolate, and the cave of depression becomes our dwelling place. Before you take another step or make another decision, ask yourself these questions:

- Did I make a hasty decision?
- Did I decide in prayer or fear?
- Am I running from responsibility?
- Where am I running to?
- Will I end up in the cave of depression?

The safest place to live is in the will of God, but it takes faith and courage to reside there. Remember, "the name of the

Depressed Mood

LORD is a strong tower"; we run to His name and are safe (Proverbs 18:10). When we push away our own understanding and acknowledge God, He will direct our paths (Proverbs 3:5–6). God is so gracious that you can seek Him now and He will guide.

One of the most commonly recognized symptoms of major depression is a depressed mood. A depressed mood speaks to how someone feels. We can see it in their countenance. The person's facial expression can appear flat, with a lack of emotion. There may be an avoidance of eye contact. Having a depressed mood means someone feels sad, "blue," "numb," "down in the dumps," or as if they have no feelings at all. Also, someone with a depressed mood can be irritable or "cranky"—but major depression is more serious and pervasive than just having a bad day or feeling grumpy.

With a depressed mood, there is a sense of hopelessness. While we all have days where we feel down, with major depression these feelings occur on most days for several weeks. Major life events, such as a death, divorce, or difficulty on a job, can be catalysts for depression and serve as fuel for these symptoms, especially if the crisis is not immediately changing in a positive direction. Seasonal changes can also affect mood. At other times, there may not be an obvious reason for a change in mood.[12][13]

Even in the trials that precipitate a depressed mood, you can have joy. With these trials, you are learning patience and perseverance (James 1:2–3). You are being strengthened in your faith. Continue to hope and God will "bless you and keep you"; He will "make His face shine upon you" and will "lift up His countenance upon you" (Numbers 6:24–26). The Lord will fill you with joy and peace as you trust in Him (Romans 15:13). Therefore, "stand firm in the faith. Be courageous. Be strong" (1 Corinthians 16:13 NLT). Your better days are closer than you think.

Another hallmark symptom of depression is anhedonia, which entails a loss of interest in activities or hobbies that used to bring someone joy. For example, someone with anhedonia would no longer have an interest in volunteering or playing card games when that sort of activity brought them a sense of pleasure in the past. Those with anhedonia may lose their "drive" and "don't care" any longer. They isolate themselves, avoiding social activities.[14][15]

> *It is not God's will that you have fear, discouragement, a depressed mood, or anhedonia.*

If you are dealing with anhedonia, it is essential to challenge yourself to communicate and socialize with others. Although you yourself long for encouragement, speak well of others; encourage and bless them with your words. Remember, "kind words are like honey—sweet to the soul and healthy for the body" (Proverbs 16:24 NLT). As you encourage others, it will encourage you. Surround yourself with believers and people of faith. In this way, you will receive the honey that soothes your soul. It is God's will that you enjoy each day (Psalm 118:24). Regardless of how you feel, or your level of desire, take a walk each morning, take yourself out to dinner, and watch a sunrise. Push past anhedonia and enjoy the beauty in the simple wonders around you.

It is not God's will that you have fear, discouragement, a depressed mood, or anhedonia. The miracle of the rain not only ended a drought and a season of famine for the people of Israel, but it also validated Elijah as the prophet of God. In like manner, God has miracles for your future that will both help others and validate you as His child.

Realize that not everyone will celebrate your validation, even when God uses you to bless them. Not everyone will speak favorable words about you as you serve God. Yet, take heart and be encouraged! God is still with you. The threat seems imminent, powerful, and dangerous, but it will not come near you. Therefore, have no fear. Make a conscious effort to reset your expectations accordingly.

Specifically, have a joyful expectancy for your promised future, which is just over the horizon. Your trials will pass. Your troubles will not last forever. Remember, "this is the day the LORD has made; we will rejoice and be glad in it" (Psalm 118:24). In your awareness of your depressed mood, give thanks to God for a future filled with joy, laughter, and good times. Gives thanks to God although you see no change in your condition. Thank Him although you may not desire to speak words of gratitude. The weapons of faith, worship, and thanksgiving for a future you have not seen hold great power when deployed in your lowest-feeling moments.

Since words of thanks are a weapon, wield your sword with courage as you battle depression and anhedonia! Despite your circumstances, make a commitment to sing songs of worship and to dance daily. In heartfelt song, your sorrows cannot find you. As you dance before the Lord, your worries will fall away. You will enjoy life again. God will strengthen you. Hope will arise in your heart day by day, and you'll imagine your life being better. Encourage others, and soon you will find encouragement with sweet words that bring you out of isolation and into a life filled with great promise.

God will break every feeling of depression and replace it with joy as you come to know Jesus and appreciate His love and sacrifice for you. Accept Him into your heart and He will change your life. You will find "the joy of the LORD is your strength" (Nehemiah 8:10). Trust in Him. Do not surrender your songs of joy.

Song of the Day:
"Joy"
by Housefires.[16]

REFLECTIONS

Day One Reflections

Question: Define what depression feels like for you. How are your mood and outlook currently?

_____
_____
_____
_____
_____
_____
_____
_____
_____
_____

Question: Reflect on recent difficult moments in your life and write down how you have responded to each of these. Did you decide to act in faith or fear?

_____
_____
_____
_____
_____
_____
_____
_____
_____
_____
_____
_____
_____
_____
_____
_____
_____
_____
_____
_____

Application: Read Psalm 118:24. Then, complete the following statement: "I find joy in…"

_____
_____
_____
_____
_____
_____
_____
_____
_____
_____
_____
_____
_____
_____
_____
_____
_____

Day One Notes

"But he himself went a day's journey into the wilderness, and came and sat down under a broom tree. And he prayed that he might die, and said," It is enough! Now, Lord, take my life, for I am no better than my fathers!"

1 KINGS 19:4

DAY TWO

Reject Thoughts of Death: Overcome and Live

Depression wasted no time in taking a drastic turn. After Elijah traveled through the wilderness alone, he came to sit under a broom tree. He prayed, but this was not a prayer of faith: Elijah prayed he might die. Overwhelmed and disheartened, Elijah was at the end of his rope. In his mind, he had reached his limits. He had walked a difficult path, including battles that had killed other prophets of the Lord, and Israel had fallen further into idol worship. He had prayed, believed, and waited for the miracle of the rain, yet a threat from Jezebel brought Elijah to a breaking point, where the weight of his emotions overtook him.

Elijah grabbed hold of a sense of worthlessness, believing he was no better than his fathers before him. He devalued his purpose and his very life. The faithful, influential, and trusted prophet of Israel abandoned not only his responsibility to help others hear the voice of God but also his desire to live. Instead of speaking words of life and faith, Elijah spoke words of death and worthlessness. In reality, Jezebel's threats would never come to pass; Elijah would continue to perform many miracles and would find a friend and helper in Elisha. In this moment, though, his bright future escaped his gaze.

There are moments in our lives that tip us over the edge into a valley of depression. It is usually not one event but an accumulation of insults, setbacks, and losses that causes someone to become weary and discouraged. These circumstances may tempt us to isolate ourselves and devalue our very life. We may think passive thoughts of not wanting to live. Like Elijah, some people may also verbalize a desire to die.

One of the most infamous symptoms of depression is having thoughts of harming oneself. The DSM-5 refers to this as suicidal ideation, or passive thoughts of harming oneself. These passive thoughts can lead progressively to verbal expressions or actions of harm.[17][18]

In the war against depression, these thoughts of death or lack of desire to live may come early in the battle as the enemy of your soul raises the stakes, attempting to cancel your joyful, accomplishment-filled future with a single, quick strike. Whenever such thoughts arise, it is apparent you have entered a thought pattern that is not of God. It is important to shut the door on these thoughts immediately. Recognize the voice of the enemy and reject it!

Arise with thanksgiving and worship instead. Call yourself

blessed and favored. Whenever you begin to speak death to yourself, speak life and call your future into existence as if it were already here (Romans 4:17). Through Jesus, you are powerful, valuable, and forgiven. Walk in this new life and cast away every argument or thought that says otherwise (2 Corinthians 10:5). Take hold of a spirit of expectation and you will feel your hope rise again.

The DSM-5 notes that feelings of guilt and worthlessness are symptoms of depression as well.[19][20] When life become difficult and we are weary with setbacks, we may feel worthless, as if our action and efforts have no effect. We may feel as though we are not useful to others. Comparison also worsens feelings of worthlessness. We can associate guilt with thoughts of past perceived failures. Again, the thoughts or words we speak can fuel a sense of worthlessness as we say to ourselves or within our hearts, "You always mess up," or, "You will never be good enough."

Remember, as followers of Jesus Christ, we listen to His voice alone and not to the words of a stranger (see John 10:27). Do not give these thoughts a moment to take root! Instead, keep your gaze on the promises of God. The thoughts that God has toward you are not to harm you, but "to give you a future and a hope" (Jeremiah 29:11)—and your future is calling you to live.

> *Intentionally decide to rest in the thoughts God has for you.*

Guarding your thoughts will help ensure your words and actions reflect faith and remain in alignment with God's plan for your life. The Bible reminds us to protect our heart because everything flows through it (Proverbs 4:23), including our thoughts, words, and actions. Make a commitment to imagine your life better.

It may be difficult to see reconciliation during a bitter divorce. Thoughts of companionship may be hard to fathom in a long season of singlehood. A life filled with financial resources can be difficult to imagine in the middle of bankruptcy. A life where you help others break free from addiction is hard to contemplate when you continue to struggle with substance abuse. A loving family sitting around a dinner table is hard to visualize when the people in a broken home no longer speak to one another or a child has left in rebellion.

Intentionally decide to rest in the thoughts God has for you. His thoughts toward you are as many as the sand on the seashore (Psalm 139:17–18). God desires to fill your future with restoration, companionship, and financial sufficiency. You will break free from every addiction. God will save your family, and you will enjoy each other's company again. Life is worth living. Your future is worth imagining.

Tell yourself you are loved, useful, and a great help to others. Remind yourself you are blessed, gifted, and favored by God. You are appreciated. Others depend on you, and the world is awaiting your gifts. All things will work to your benefit as you serve God (Romans 8:28).

There is no need to compare yourself to others, because you are "fearfully and wonderfully made" (Psalm 139:14). God knows the very number of hairs upon your head (Luke 12:7). He made no mistakes when He created you. Characteristics you may find unattractive about yourself, such as your speech, height, or personality, God loves. You are unique. Your value to God is beyond anything you can imagine. He exchanged His life for yours so that you may be free from condemnation, guilt, or feelings of worthlessness. Therefore, reject guilt and condemnation as you walk in the Spirit (Romans 8:1). Let your confidence be in the Lord alone (see Jeremiah 17:7).

Realize that God remains close in your trials and moves in the quiet moments. When you feel God is far away, He is closer than you would ever imagine. When you feel unheard, Jesus understands, and He is listening and praying for you (see Hebrews 4:15, 7:25). When you feel your words and actions have no impact, you are destroying barriers and breaking strongholds beyond what you can see with your natural eyes. How do you know that your words or actions have not empowered someone to change the trajectory of their life?

Before you address your self-worth, ask yourself these questions:

- Can I look into the heart of another?
- Am I comparing myself to others?
- What are my unique talents?
- What are my accomplishments, or proof that God has walked with and validated me?
- What does God say about my worth?
- Are these feelings of worthless from God or the enemy?

Like Elijah, you have great promise and talents that God will use for His kingdom. With great promise come mighty attacks on your thoughts and sense of worth, so focus on the miracles and pay attention to your accomplishments. Give thanks to God in advance for your redemptive future. When emotions tell you, "I have reached my limit," realize God created you and knows how much you can carry. He pushes us to be stronger but also takes over when circumstances press us beyond our strength (see 2 Corinthians 1:8). When we are ready to "throw in the towel" or "raise the white flag," God gives us rest and strength, sending us back into the ring or onto the battlefield to accomplish a victory for His glory.

You are stronger than you know, more resilient than you realize—talented, gifted, and influential. Take confidence in knowing "the battle is not yours, but God's" (2 Chronicles 20:15). Instead of focusing on thoughts of defeat, fill your imagination with thoughts of your future. Your friends and family are awaiting your presence. They long to hear your laughter. Others are waiting to invest in your business or read your book. Some are waiting to hear the story of your restored life so that it may encourage them.

The enemy wants nothing more for you than to focus on a negative image of your life that does not reflect reality. Your adversary wants you to fix your eyes on a lie so that you would contemplate and speak defeat. Knowing this, refuse to speak death or defeat. Don't even think about such things! Reject all feelings of worthlessness that try to latch onto you as leeches, draining your blood, energy, and motivation. Do not become weary in doing the right thing, because your future life is amazing and closer than you think (see Galatians 6:9)!

Instead, think those things that are true, just, lovely, and "of a good report" (Philippians 4:8). Forget the setbacks, and focus on the future. Let the negative thoughts fade away. Let the words of your mouth and the meditation of your heart be acceptable to God (Psalm 19:14). Destroy thoughts of death and replace them with a desire to live. Reverse your feelings of worthlessness and guilt, experiencing instead the truth of your great value to God.

As you turn the tide of your thoughts, your groans will transform into praise. When you lock your eyes on Jesus and His extravagant love for you, there will be no room left for vain imaginations, defeat, or lies. Acknowledging your worth, and that Jesus took all your guilt, step forward in freedom!

Song of the Day:
"When I Lock Eyes on You/
Your Love Is Extravagant"
by Harvest.[21]

RESOURCES

National Suicide Prevention Helpline

If you are considering harming yourself or anyone else, it is important that you speak with someone right away. The National Suicide Prevention Helpline connects you with a crisis center in your area. You can talk about anything: your thoughts, feelings, concerns, or painful memories. You need someone who serves simply to listen. Even if you have no thoughts of hurting yourself, you can still call the hotline (800-273-8255). There is no judgment, shame, or fear involved in calling the hotline to speak with someone to help guide you through your thoughts.

You can find more information at:
https://suicidepreventionlifeline.org/talk-to-someone-now/.

REFLECTIONS

Day Two Reflections

Question: What do you love about yourself, and what does God love about you? Read Jeremiah 29:11. What might a better future look like for you?

_____
_____
_____
_____
_____
_____
_____
_____

Question: How can you be proactive in your own progression? Write out a prayer for God's support on your journey out of depression.

_____

_____
_____
_____
_____
_____
_____
_____
_____
_____
_____
_____
_____
_____
_____
_____
_____
_____
_____
_____
_____

Question: Read Psalm 139:17–18. Then, complete the following statement: "I am thankful to God for..."

Day Two Notes

"Then as he lay and slept under the broom tree, suddenly an angel touched him, and said to him, "Arise and eat."

1 KINGS 19:5

DAY THREE

Loss of Appetite: Arise and Eat

Elijah traveled though the wilderness alone. By choice, he was away from the support of his servant. In a reflexive, impulsive decision in response to a threatening message from Jezebel, Elijah ran down a path of despair.

He came to sleep under a broom tree. Watered by discouragement, seeds of worthlessness took root. Depression was in full bloom. Worse, in his depression, Elijah was not eating; it seems he had failed to bring the necessary rations or supplies. He prayed that he might die, but God was close with comfort and provision.

Suddenly, an angel awakened him. Elijah never asked for a meal, but God knew his needs. While the prophet was resting, God was preparing a blessing to refresh him. The angel told Elijah to arise and eat. Belatedly, Elijah recognized that his body must receive sustenance.

Even in the wilderness, God is patient with our frustration and proves himself to be Jehovah Jireh—our provider. Like Elijah, in times of depression, you might travel unprepared in the wilderness of despair. You may separate yourself from the support of your family and friends. While walking in a direction opposite your responsibility, you might put off praying for others, volunteering at homeless shelters, or calling an elderly friend.

When depressed, you may also neglect your health by eating too much or not enough. Depression can produce a ripple effect whereby your mental health affects your physical health. According to the DSM-5, changes in appetite and weight can be a symptom of depression. Consumed with emotions, you may lose your desire to eat. Emotional hurt sometimes supersedes the pain of hunger, as days pass by without you eating sufficiently. As a result, some people with severe depression can lose a significant amount of weight.

On the other hand, as a comfort measure, some with depression can eat more than normal or make unhealthy food choices. You may have cravings for junk food, such as candy bars, ice cream, or potato chips. If someone struggles with making healthy food choices already, it can worsen during periods of depression. Significant weight gain therefore accompanies depression for some people.[22][23]

While there can be a multitude of reasons for your eating patterns to change, it is important to be aware of both your physical and mental needs. You need to nourish your body,

LOSS OF APPETITE

despite depression. Be aware of your emotions, but do not let them drive your decisions, including food choices. Such decisions can worsen blood pressure, high cholesterol, or diabetes control. And regardless of your eating or weight changes, believe that God loves you and has an amazing plan for your life (see Jeremiah 29:11).

When your mental health influences your dietary choices, it doesn't just have repercussions on your physical health: the physical effects, in turn, can further harm your mental well-being. Research shows that those with a combination of high blood pressure, obesity, and high cholesterol have more difficulty recovering from depression.[24] By contrast, studies have shown, a healthy diet can prevent the onset of depressive symptoms.[25][26]

Therefore, it is important to stop depression in its tracks by eating regularly and making conscientious food choices. Arm yourself with knowledge about which foods can improve your energy levels, such as fruits and vegetables, and which foods can cause you to feel sluggish, such as those high in carbohydrates and unhealthy fats. Remember the proverb, "An intelligent heart acquires knowledge, and the ear of the wise seeks knowledge" (Proverbs 18:15 ESV). Therefore, learn all you can about the foods you should eat to keep yourself healthy and free of disease.

Rise above depression by deciding to eat a well-balanced diet. In this way, you can remain healthy and possess your promise with strength and vitality when it arrives. Bring yourself the joy of eating with gladness, and prepare your heart for dreams to come. If you notice you have lost weight, experience a decreased appetite, or lack the desire to eat, make a commitment to eat more regularly while giving thanks to God. If you notice weight gain or a tendency to crave unhealthy foods, glorify God by making healthy food choices to better care for God's temple, your body. When you make dietary decisions that reflect your value for life and appreciation of all things that God provides, you can rule over your depression.

> *Without asking, you will awaken, look up, and see your provision.*

God wants you to partake in all the joys in life, including eating meals. Do not allow depression to take a foothold in your physical health; instead, eat and drink with a glad heart (Ecclesiastes 9:7). Not only will you break the chains of depression, but you will also enjoy all the things God created, including meals eaten with gratitude. As you move away from isolation, "arise and eat": bring yourself back to your support circle and break bread with them continually, receiving strength and encouragement (see Acts 2:42).

God knows your troubles. His compassion and provision are close—and He knows your needs even before you ask (Matthew 6:8). He is your Jireh, who longs to provide for you. Even if, like Elijah, you have taken a detour down a path of depression, Jesus will not condemn you (Romans 8:1) but will prepare a blessing to strengthen you for the journey ahead. Without asking, you will awaken, look up, and see your provision.

Song of the Day:
"Jireh"
by Elevation Worship
and Maverick City.[27]

Resources

Mediterranean Diet

The Mediterranean eating plan is a broad term used to describe a type of eating pattern practiced by those who live along the Mediterranean Sea. The Mediterranean eating plan uses olive oil as the primary fat source. People who follow this plan consume dairy, eggs, and fish in modest amounts, while there are generous amounts of fruits, vegetables, beans, and whole grains.

For more information, visit:
https://www.heart.org/en/healthy-living/healthy-eating/eat-smart/nutrition-basics/mediterranean-diet.

DASH Diet

The DASH eating plan stands for Dietary Approaches to Stop Hypertension. This eating plan lowers blood pressure and focuses on limiting red meat, salt, sweets, and added sugars.

For more information, visit the National Institute of Health:

https://www.nhlbi.nih.gov/files/docs/public/heart/hbp_low.pdf.

Plant-Based Diet

A plant-based eating plan can vary and include those who are strictly vegan—which is an entirely plant-based diet, as those who are vegan typically avoid all meats, diary, and eggs. On the other end of the spectrum, those who are plant-forward will eat meat, yet the main staples of their meals are plants. Vegetarians will exclude meat from their diet but may eat diary and eggs. There is good evidence for a plant-based diet, or an eating plan mostly focused on plant-based foods.

To find out more, visit the American Heart Association:

https://www.heart.org/en/healthy-living/healthy-eating/eat-smart/nutrition-basics/how-does-plant-forward-eating-benefit-your-health.

Heart Healthy Diet

The Heart Healthy eating plan has similar features to the DASH, Mediterranean, and plant-based diet, with a focus on eating a diet rich in fruits, vegetables, whole grains, and skinless poultry and fish. Dairy consumed should be low in fat. There should also be a limit on salt, red meat, sweets, and foods with saturated or trans fats.

For more information, visit the American Heart Association:

https://www.heart.org/en/health-topics/high-blood-pressure/changes-you-can-make-to-manage-high-blood-pressure/managing-blood-pressure-with-a-heart-healthy-diet.

REFLECTIONS

Day Three Reflections

Question: Use the resources and research healthy eating. What changes could you make to your diet to aid your recovery from depression?

_____
_____
_____
_____
_____
_____
_____
_____
_____

Question: Read Acts 2:42. How will you bring yourself back from isolation?

Question: Read Ecclesiastes 9:7. Then, complete the following statement: "God has provided for me by…"

Day Three Notes

"Then he looked, and there by his head was a cake baked on coals, and a jar of water. So he ate and drank, and lay down again."

1 KINGS 19:6

DAY FOUR

Disturbances of Sleep and Concentration: Awake and Move

On the heels of a great miracle whereby a three-year drought had ended, a threat from Jezebel had sent Elijah into a tailspin of discouragement. This unfulfilled threat tipped him into a whirlpool of choices, down a path of despair, and into a cave of depression.

When you grab hold of an assignment or responsibility from God, maybe you are unaware of the opposition or tribulation that accompanies this choice. Yet, God knows. He is ready to prepare and strengthen you for the journey, even if you stray temporarily off the path of the promise.

Alone and unprepared, Elijah experienced a depressed mood. Feelings of worthlessness had encompassed him, and he confessed his thoughts of not wanting to live. Elijah was in a physical and mental wilderness. Still, God did not condemn him. Elijah had not eaten at first, but while he was resting, God had prepared a meal of cake and water to strengthen him. Fortunately, Elijah ate; he did not reject the food he needed to sustain himself.

Yet, instead of continuing in his journey or turning back to the promise of God, Elijah lay down again. Depression paralyzed him, leaving him unable to move as he fell asleep once more. He was in a repetitive sleep cycle.

If you travel the road of depression long enough, you can come to a point in time where you become stagnant in your movement. Even in the absence of depression, you need to have an appropriate amount of rest. When depression sets in, sometimes you may sleep too much. You may become less productive and lose focus on the work ahead.

Instead of getting to work early and performing your job with diligence, you might oversleep or coast through your work day on mediocre effort. Rather than accomplish a dream, such as starting a business or writing a book, and share your gifts with the world, you may doze your days away. In place of calling your friends and family to encourage them, maybe you take naps. God desires to use your life purposefully to build up His kingdom and encourage others (see Ephesians 4:12). Yet, with depression, you can find yourself consumed with the busyness of sleeping.

The DSM-5 notes that changes in sleep patterns are a characteristic of major depression.[28][29] Someone can either sleep too much or not enough. While sleep may provide an escape from persistent thoughts of your present reality, at other times recurrent thoughts of painful memories and past experiences can keep you awake at night. Even when those with depression have adequate sleep, they may not feel rested. They may stay up all night or fall back to sleep upon awakening in the morning. Those with depression may feel as though they do not want to rise out of bed.

Poor sleep can affect your thought patterns, resulting in poor concentration. Even when sleep is adequate, poor concentration can result from depression. You may complain of memory difficulties and have trouble making decisions or focusing on tasks. And, as in the story of Elijah, those with depression may enter a sleep/eat cycle, finding comfort in alternately eating and sleeping.

Jesus has vindication, validation, and victory for your future.

Understandably, sometimes sleep may be the only time when thoughts of past harms, present troubles, or future threats do not consume your mind. But there is no need to escape your present reality. We know God fights all our battles (Deuteronomy 3:22). What you see with your natural eyes is distinct from what occurs in the Spirit (see 2 Kings 6:16–18).

The Spirit seals and fulfills God's promises to you.

Acknowledge your stagnation, but purpose in your heart to move toward God with vigor. A life filled with purpose and meaningful accomplishments is calling to you. You are free to rejoice in this moment, believing in God's promises and rejecting what you see with your eyes. Awaken and live! Your future awaits you expectantly.

At other times, racing thoughts may keep you up at night. Maybe you give too much thought to the past, rehashing hurtful memories and the words you should have said or things you should have done in those past situations. You might rehearse in your mind for a chance encounter with a friend who once betrayed you but you haven't seen in years. Thoughts of attempted solutions to your financial troubles or concerns about your children's future can pace endlessly and fruitlessly in your mind in the nighttime hours.

But remember, you are to be anxious for nothing! You are to pray and make your requests known to God so that you can guard your heart and mind and experience true peace (Philippians 4:6–7). Despite all the trouble and concerns that are keeping you up at night, none of this worry can add an hour to your life (Luke 12:25 NIV). God has already made provisions and a path to deliver you from all your troubles. "Do not be afraid; only believe" (Mark 5:36).

Rather than attempt to escape your troubles, or to comfort yourself through overeating or oversleeping, bring all your cares to God so that He may fix them permanently and comfort you. Remember, you serve the "God of all comfort"

(2 Corinthians 1:3), who "comforts us in all our troubles so that we can comfort others" (2 Corinthians 1:4 NLT). God has given you strength to face your reality, and He supplies you with peace in the midst of your troubles. Whether you are sleeping too much or not enough, God will give you rest. He will strengthen and encourage you as you remember, "God gives rest to his loved ones" (Psalm 127:2 NLT).

When you believe the threats of your present, it leads you to believe the lie of a future filled with defeat. Reject the lies of defeat, and accept the truth that Jesus has vindication, validation, and victory for your future. Keeping your attention on the promises of God can help you gain fresh insight into your condition and cultivate a drive to accomplish your dreams. Knowing that Jesus is with you in the moments of your depression is your reassurance that you will make it out of this wilderness whole and on your way to a better life.

Make a commitment to awaken with joy in your heart and thanksgiving on your lips in the morning hours. Enjoy quiet time with Jesus or take an early walk outside instead of going back to sleep. Change your focus from your circumstances and enjoy the world around you as you rise above depression.

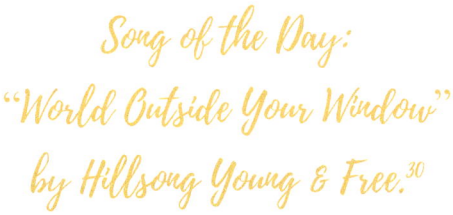

Song of the Day:
"World Outside Your Window"
by Hillsong Young & Free.[30]

RESOURCES

American Thoracic Society

The American Thoracic Society provides great recommendations and resources for sleep medicine. You can find a helpful handout on healthy sleep in adults on the American Thoracic Society website.

For more information, visit: https://www.thoracic.org/patients/patient-resources/resources/healthy-sleep-in-adults.pdf.

REFLECTIONS

Day Four Reflections

Question: According to Psalm 127:2, why does God want you to rest? Are you sleeping too much or not enough? If you're sleeping too much, what troubles or thoughts do you wish to escape through excessive sleep? If you're not sleeping enough, what concerns keep you up at night?

_____
_____
_____
_____
_____
_____
_____
_____

Question: Make a plan to sleep in a healthy way. What are your present threats? How do they impact your view of your future? When sleeping, do you feel rested? Why or why not? Read Luke 12:25, and pray for your fears and worries. Ask God for strength for the battle ahead.

Question: With Philippians 4:6–7 in mind, write a statement about the specific cares you will give to God today:

_____
_____
_____
_____
_____
_____
_____
_____
_____
_____
_____
_____
_____
_____
_____
_____
_____
_____
_____

Day Four Notes

"And the angel of the Lord came back the second time, and touched him, and said, "Arise and eat, because the journey is too great for you." So he arose, and ate and drank; and he went in the strength of that food forty nights as far as Horeb, the mountain of God."

1 KINGS 19:7-8

DAY FIVE

Tiredness, Fatigue, and Psychomotor Changes: Go in Strength

Elijah was stagnant, caught in a sleep/eat cycle that sought to paralyze his progress. Overwhelmed and exhausted, he experienced a sense of physical and emotional fatigue. But God was aware of Elijah's need for food and strength in preparation for the journey ahead. The angel, who had already acknowledged the prophet's hunger and fatigue, came to Elijah a second time and reminded him again to eat. Whether he knew it or not, Elijah did not have enough strength to endure his journey into the cave of depression.

Even after he ate and drank to bolster his strength, Elijah declined to return directly to confront Jezebel: he undertook a forty-day journey to the mountain of God. Instead of rebuking the prophet for traveling his own way, God plotted Elijah's way to the cave of depression—and, from there, his return to the heart of God's plan for him.

This point in Elijah's journey brings us to an important realization about God: Jesus is aware of our fatigue and limitations, and He provides strength for our travels, even those that seem in the moment to run counter to His will. Remember, "we know God causes everything to work together for the good of those who love God and are called according to his purpose for them" (Romans 8:28 NLT).

The DSM-5 lists feelings of fatigue, or tiredness, as another symptom of depression.[31][32] Understandably, changes in sleep patterns can affect one's energy level. Beyond this, people with depression can become easily exhausted with simple tasks and feel the need to rest frequently during the day. They can feel "weighed down" and "heavy." This fatigue can persist throughout the day. Because of this fatigue, those with depression may not even have the energy to clean their home or bathe themselves properly. Simple tasks seem to cause great exhaustion.

On the one hand, those suffering depression may also experience psychomotor retardation, which is the slowing of body movements. People with psychomotor retardation may speak or think slowly, feeling sluggish. Everyday actions and movements, such as preparing coffee, happen at a slowed pace. On the other hand, depression may cause psychomotor agitation, which is the speeding up of body movements. Those with psychomotor agitation may appear to be fidgety, or they may pace with worry.

The bottom line is, with inadequate rest and a poor appetite, fatigue and exhaustion are soon to follow. Fatigue increasingly paralyzes your movement, as you become too tired to clean your home, exercise, or make your way to church or social gatherings. It can serve to isolate you further, because you become too tired to interact with others. Even when you are among others, a sense of tiredness may weigh you down.

But fatigue and exhaustion will have no effect on you when you rely on God to restore your soul and lead you on a righteous path "for His name's sake" (Psalm 23:3). Sluggishness and agitation will fall away as you give thanks for the day the Lord has made (Psalm 118:24).

> *Let us do what we can.*
> *God will carry us*
> *the rest of the way.*

Although you may feel tired and weighed down, make a conscious decision to take a walk outside and enjoy the wind on your face or the smell of fresh air. God gave us many tools to improve our mood, including eating a healthy diet and exercising. Even if you feel sluggish, exercise regularly. Not only is exercise a key component to overall good health, but it has also been shown to improve your mood. Regular exercise helps with diabetes and blood pressure control, and research shows it alleviates the symptoms of depression.[33] [34] [35] Exercise releases hormones called endorphins, which act on the brain to decrease pain and stress and increase happiness.[36]

When you finish enjoying the weather and exercising, consider buying a new outfit and taking yourself out to dinner. In doing this, you will uplift your emotions and feel a sense of accomplishment. You will be glad you pushed past fatigue and sluggishness and learned to appreciate the simple things in life.

It requires a conscious effort to take advantage of what God has given you. Do what you can, and God will carry you the rest of the way. Jesus cares about your rest, as well as about your sustenance to endure life's travels. Have no fear, for you know God will strengthen and uphold you with His righteous right hand (Isaiah 41:10). He will bring you back to His promise, even if you need to take a detour first.

Remember, "the LORD lifts up those who are weighed down" (Psalm 146:8 NLT). Let God lift you above your depression, that you may see the beauty of life. He will satisfy your weary soul and replenish you (Jeremiah 31:25), because He desires for you to have a fulfilling life. His plans for you are not to harm you, but to give you hope for the future. It is in this promised future that you can rejoice now!

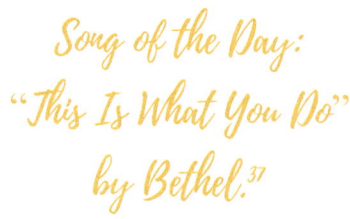

Song of the Day:
"This Is What You Do"
by Bethel.[37]

RESOURCES

American Heart Association

The American Heart Association provides excellent exercise recommendations for both children and adults. Adults should aim for 150 minutes of moderate activity per week. This is a kind of activity where you will break a sweat, but it is not considered vigorous. You can divide this weekly activity into fifty minutes, three times a week, or thirty minutes, five times a week. You can add strength training at least twice a week for further benefit. As you work exercise into your daily routine, you will feel and look better.

For more information, visit the American Heart Association website.

https://www.heart.org/en/healthy-living/fitness/fitness-basics/aha-recs-for-physical-activity-in-adults.

REFLECTIONS

Day Five Reflections

Question: Are you easily exhausted? How has this affected your daily habits? Are you caring for yourself, cleaning your home, and talking with friends? How is your performance at work impacted? Explain in detail.

_____
_____
_____
_____
_____
_____
_____
_____

Question: What detours have you taken on your journey? Have you allowed God to guide you back to your path? How are you making a conscious effort to embrace what's been given to you?

_____
_____
_____
_____
_____
_____
_____
_____
_____
_____
_____
_____
_____
_____
_____
_____
_____
_____

Question: Read Psalm 146:8 and Jeremiah 31:25. Then, create a daily devotional schedule to help God lift you up and replenish you, listing books and chapters of interest in the Bible as well as songs of worship that will strengthen you:

_____
_____
_____
_____
_____
_____
_____
_____
_____
_____
_____
_____
_____
_____
_____
_____
_____
_____
_____
_____

Day Five Notes

"And there he went into a cave, and spent the night in that place; and behold, the word of the Lord came to him, and He said to him, "What are you doing here, Elijah?"

"So he said, "I have been zealous for the Lord God of hosts; for the children of Israel have forsaken Your covenant, torn down Your altars, and killed Your prophets with the sword. I alone am left; and they seek to take my life."

1 KINGS 19:9-10

DAY SIX

Worthlessness and Guilt: What Are You Doing Here?

With the miracle of the rain came an end both to the drought and to a famine that had caused great suffering in Israel. Yet it seems Elijah's suffering was only beginning. The prophet finished his journey of despair and arrived in a cave of depression. He now found himself further isolated in a dark place where others could not find him. In addition to being discouraged, Elijah felt depressed and fatigued. His words reflected death and defeat. He slept too much and did not eat.

But God, ever patient, remained nearby. Although Elijah sought to be alone, he could not run from the compassion of God. As the prophet wallowed in the depth of his despair, God spoke to him, called him by name, and asked a simple question: "What are you doing here?"

Now we finally get the reason Elijah ran away. He told God

about his zealous works, but he also revealed the mistaken perception that he was the last prophet in Israel. This misperception was not reality; it was a false image that had consumed Elijah's thoughts. He had entered a rabbit hole of self-defeating thoughts that did not reflect the real world.

Similarly, when you process your perceptions through a discouragement-fueled engine of human reasoning, your feelings toward your present circumstance are far from reality. You may operate in extremes and believe no one else has experienced your level of hurt or abandonment.

The DSM-5 describes feelings of worthlessness and guilt as symptoms of depression.[38][39] Feelings of worthlessness can permeate your thoughts as you dwell on past failures and delayed successes. Those who have feelings of worthlessness can perceive themselves as inferior to others. Such comparisons to other, successful-seeming individuals fuels a sense of inadequacy. You may tend to magnify minor setbacks.

Somehow, too, you may feel punished or condemned for a sin of your past. Instead of believing in the promises of God, you might rest on falsehoods and lies about your present circumstances and your future.

The Bible tells us that "no temptation that has overtaken you except such as is common to man" and that God will "make the way of escape, that you may be able to bear it" (1 Corinthians 10:13). Therefore, you can bear your difficulties knowing that God provides a way to escape from your depression, with belief in His word and His promises for your future. Remember, "if anyone is in Christ, he is a new creation; old things have passed away (2 Corinthians 5:17a). Decide today to believe that God loves you and holds an amazing future in His hands that no one can take away.

Instead of focusing on threats of losing a job, family member, or marriage, bring yourself back to reality and recognize that Jesus has redemptive power to give you a better job, intact family, and restored marriage. Even though you may want to run from your assignment, it does not mean you should run from the presence of God. In fact, in His presence, you can submit your disappointments, confusion, misunderstanding, and hurt and, in return, receive encouragement, truth, and direction. So continue to pray, continue to go to church, and continue in your morning devotionals.

Exaggerated perceptions of your troubles may cause you to believe no one cares for you or that God Himself has forgotten your prayers. At other times, you may believe you can hide from God, when in truth, "the LORD your God will personally go ahead of you. He will neither fail you nor abandon you" (Deuteronomy 31:6 NLT). There is nowhere you can escape God, even if you go to the ends of the earth (Psalm 139:7–10). Even though you may not have the power to change your situation, you have the opportunity to trust in Jesus for the miraculous.

> *God listens and reorients us to the truth in place of our perceptions.*

You might feel a sense of worthlessness when you cannot change your situation, and you might experience guilt when it seems your contributions to the kingdom of God have not been impactful. But God reorients us to the truth in place of faulty perceptions like these. Elijah despaired that he was alone, yet his servant Elisha was waiting expectantly, and other prophets Elijah did not know of likewise refused to bow to Baal. Do not judge your situation on what you do not see, but believe God has you on His mind and will deliver you!

Don't forget the promises God spoke to you before you entered a marriage now headed toward divorce or a dream job you are now at risk of losing. God honors marriage (Hebrews 13:4). You will be the head and not the tail (Deuteronomy 28:13). Above all, believe that there is no condemnation for "those who are in Christ Jesus" and walk by the Spirit (Romans 8:1). The blood of Jesus is enough to wipe away the sins of your past, so God will not punish you after your heart has turned in His direction.

God's thoughts toward you are not to harm you but "to give you a future and a hope" (Jeremiah 29:11). The promises do not change just because your life has entered a season of difficulty. You are coming out of your depression stronger, wiser,

WORTHLESSNESS/GUILT

and equipped to help others defeat this giant as well. Jesus is "interceding" (praying) for you (Romans 8:34). Stand behind Him as He fights your battle and defeats every negative emotion, thought, or inclination! Jesus is your champion, who has defeated hell, the grave, and death, and He will defeat your depression as well.

Song of the Day:
"Emmanuel (Champion of the World)"
by Upper Room.[40]

REFLECTIONS

Day Six Reflections

Question: Who is in your support circle? Write their names here.

_____
_____
_____
_____
_____
_____
_____
_____
_____

Question: Are there people you want to reach out to on your journey? Write their names here.

_____
_____
_____
_____
_____
_____
_____
_____
_____
_____
_____
_____
_____
_____
_____
_____
_____
_____
_____
_____

Question: Unburden yourself to God. Let go of self-doubt, guilt, and negativity. Leave them on this page and let God bring you encouragement and direction. Complete the statement: "I'm letting go of…"

_____
_____
_____
_____
_____
_____
_____
_____
_____
_____
_____
_____
_____
_____
_____
_____
_____
_____
_____
_____
_____

Day Six Notes

" Then He said, "Go out, and stand on the mountain before the Lord." And behold, the Lord passed by, and a great and strong wind tore into the mountains and broke the rocks in pieces before the Lord, but the Lord was not in the wind; and after the wind an earthquake, but the Lord was not in the earthquake;"

" and after the earthquake a fire, but the Lord was not in the fire; and after the fire a still small voice."

1 KINGS 19:11-12

DAY SEVEN

Still, Small Voice: Your New Life Awaits

Elijah had arrived at Mount Horeb, or Sinai, referred to as the mountain of God. This mountain had great significance, as an angel of the Lord once appeared to Moses in a burning bush near Mount Sinai, instructing him to return to Egypt. Later, when the children of Israel left Egypt, they camped at the foot of Sinai. Moses also ascended this mountain to communicate with God and receive the Ten Commandments.

God spoke to Elijah on this same mountain, revealing the truth of his current reality to him, just as Moses had received revelation about the will of God for the people of Israel. Though Elijah ran from his responsibility after receiving a threat from Jezebel, he did not run away from God but intentionally traveled to a mountain of revelation. In a similar manner, in all your troubles, you ought to hasten to the cross, into the presence of God. In this way, you will receive truth, encouragement, revelation, and explicit instructions for redirection, reconciliation, and restoration.

The voice of our all-powerful God may surprise us, but He speaks softly and leads us gently to a path that ends in joy and promise. When He first asked Elijah, "Why are you here?" He listened to Elijah's response but then instructed him to go to the entrance of the cave. Similarly, when you respond to God, you may not get a direct answer, but instead may receive an instruction to go to a place or perform an action that seems unrelated. Yet, obedience to His direction will allow you to experience Him in a new way.

Elijah was obedient. He went to the entrance of the cave—and witnessed something unexpected. As God passed by, the wind broke apart the rock on the mountains, the earth shook, and a fire burned. Then, a small whisper carried the voice of God, speaking the same question: "Why are you here?" Elijah gave the same answer as before, conveying both his zealous pursuit of God and the incorrect perceptions that he was the only prophet left in Israel and his life was in danger.

In response, this time, God gave Elijah truth and a directive (1 Kings 19:15–18): He told the prophet to return the way he had come and to anoint a new king of Syria and Israel, as well as Elisha, a new prophet. Moreover, God told Elijah of seven thousand in Israel who had a heart to serve Him, and He gave Elijah simple instructions to return to his responsibilities as a prophet.

Similarly, while you're in the presence of God, He may

direct you to return to your responsibilities—perhaps by apologizing to your boss at work or to your spouse at home. God may instruct you to rebuild a relationship bridge you have burned in the past with your harsh words or actions. The day you hear the voice of God, remember not to harden your heart (Hebrews 3:15). Listen for the words of forgiveness, reconciliation, and repentance that bring peace and restoration and lead to the heart of God.

Once you tell God how you feel, you have to be careful to listen as well. When you listen, you must pay attention to those gentle impressions, nudges, and whispers in your spirit that tell you to do something or speak a soft word. You are to be attuned to His voice, because you may not hear a thunder or a roar but a gentle voice speaking to your spirit.

Though His voice is gentle, His words and encouragement are undeniable. The presence of God strengthens you with a sense of security and vitality as you place your confidence in His direction. This gentle nudging or impression guides you down a path back to His promise.

When God speaks into your moments of difficulty and discouragement, He also addresses the actual reasons you strayed off His path of promise. His voice will speak to your true motives for getting off track. Are you more concerned about money than your marriage? Has career advancement captivated your attention instead of spending time with your family? Are you more concerned with power and prestige than with serving others? God listens to your answers, which you may rehearse and recite, but He also gives you the truth of your condition and a directive to return to His promise. The voice of God will align with His word in the Bible, and He will confirm it with your past or present experiences and observations.

We've learned that the tentacles of depression can affect our mood, desire to live, eating habits, sleep patterns, concentration, and feelings of worth(lessness) and guilt. Your night of difficulty may seem endless. Even as the sun peeks over the horizon to give a glimmer of light to a new dawn, it sometimes encourages you only for a moment as you long for more brilliant sunshine in the fullness of the day. You may feel that you cannot entertain another disappointment or hear another evil report.

Believe God will not put more on you than you can bear. Though the Bible reminds us, "He will not allow the temptation to be more than you can stand" (1 Corinthians 10:13 NLT), you will face some moments that crush you beyond your strength. Paul reminded us of this when he wrote to the church at Corinth, "We were crushed and overwhelmed beyond our ability to endure, and we thought we would never live through it." He continued, "We stopped relying on ourselves and learned to rely only on God" (2 Corinthians 1:9 NLT).

God knows your limits and what you can endure. In one sense, when you believe you can't handle any more troubles, God strengthens your endurance because He knows that when you rely on Him, you can handle and withstand more. In another sense, it would be disingenuous to say your circumstances will never crush you beyond your ability to endure or you will never despair of life itself. Reject the feeling of guilt that you have disappointed God because life overwhelmed you beyond your strength! Do not believe that God has abandoned you if you are feeling crushed. He is nearby, ready to take all your burdens so you can enter the peace that comes from trusting in Him.

> *Rejoice in your trials, knowing that God is maturing you spiritually and emotionally.*

Take hold of the opportunity to rely upon God completely when life seems overwhelming. Rejoice in your trials, knowing that God is maturing you spiritually and emotionally. Your deliverance is certain, and God will carry you through any difficulty you can imagine. Remember, as you wait on the Lord, He will renew your strength (Isaiah 40:31). He is "able to do exceedingly abundantly above all that we ask or think" (Ephesians 3:20a). The voice of God meets us in our low place and pierces the darkness. You know you cannot lift the load on your own, but Jesus is ready to come alongside you. He is waiting for you to give Him all your burdens (Matthew 11:28–30). Therefore, learn to depend completely on God for His saving power, and He will save you suddenly, mightily, and definitively!

There is freedom in resting in God and relying on Him, for "where the Spirit of the Lord is, there is liberty" (2 Corinthians 3:17). No matter how long you have been in the cave, no matter how much time has passed, you can pursue your dream again. You can pursue the plans God has for your life. Though God sometimes allows you to travel in a direction that does not seem to align with His will, you will learn from your travels to the cave of depression. Even when you believe you have control over your plans, the Lord directs your steps (Proverbs 16:9) and provides you with strength for a journey that will ultimately lead to His will.

God always knows where you are, and He has not given up on you. He knows your thoughts and empathizes with your emotions, but His voice speaks softly to your spirit, leading you to truth. With the same boldness and courage God has provided in the past to bring you to breakthroughs in your troubles, He will lead you on a path back to His will, comforting your discouragement with truth.

Knowing this, give God your burdens, "for He cares for you" (1 Peter 5:7). How do you give Him your burdens? Stop worrying. Stop thinking of the possibilities. Stop rehearsing scenarios. Let your mind be at rest. Instead, take a walk. Eat a meal alone with God. Be thankful for every success, even if a setback follows. And thank Him in advance for saving you! Even now, He is strengthening you for the new life that awaits you on a new horizon.

Song of the Day:
"New Horizon"
by Housefires.[41]

REFLECTIONS

Day Seven Reflections

Question: When you take time to hear the still, small voice of God, what do you hear? Tell God how you're feeling and listen to His response. What is He telling you? How is His Word guiding you?

_____
_____
_____
_____
_____
_____
_____
_____

Question: What is your plan for a peaceful new life? What do you currently feel God has planned for your life? What path will you need to travel down? What relationship will you need to build?

_____
_____
_____
_____
_____
_____
_____
_____
_____
_____
_____
_____
_____
_____
_____
_____
_____
_____
_____
_____

Question: Complete the following statement: "My journey looks like…"

Day Seven Notes

About the Author

JAMAL ROSS is a board-certified physician in Internal Medicine and Pediatrics. He is also a fellow of the American College of Physicians and American Academy of Pediatrics. Jamal began his career in hospital medicine and transitioned to primary care with a focus on disease prevention. Prior to medicine, Jamal works as an elementary school teacher and social worker. Through his mission work in Haiti and El Salvador, Jamal developed a desire to place prayer back into the practice of medicine and remind all that God as the Great Physician.

About Renown Publishing

Renown Publishing was founded with one mission in mind: to make your great idea famous.

At Renown Publishing, we don't just publish. We work hard to pair strategy with innovative marketing techniques so that your book launch is the start of something bigger.

Learn more at RenownPublishing.com.

REFERENCES

Notes

1. Britannica, "Elijah." By Kevin Smith. https://www.britannica.com/biography/Elijah-Hebrew-prophet.

2. Hasin, D. S., A. L. Sarvet, J. L. Meyers, T. D. Saha, W. J. Ruan, M. Stohl, and B. F. Grant. "Epidemiology of Adult DSM-5 Major Depressive Disorder and Its Specifiers in the United States." *JAMA Psychiatry* 75, no. 4 (April 1, 2018): p. 336–346.

3. Goldman, L. S., N. H. Nielsen, and H. C. Champion. "Awareness, Diagnosis, and Treatment of Depression." *J Gen Intern Med* 14, no. 9 (1999): p. 569–580. doi:10.1046/j.1525-1497.1999.03478.x.

4. Hasin, D. S., A. L. Sarvet, J. L. Meyers, T. D. Saha, W. J. Ruan, M. Stohl, and B. F. Grant. "Epidemiology of Adult DSM-5 Major Depressive Disorder and Its Specifiers in the United States." *JAMA Psychiatry* 75, no. 4 (April 1, 2018): p. 336–346.

5. Hoyt, Lynne A., Emory L. Cowen, JoAnne L. Pedro-Carroll, and Linda J. Alpert-Gillis. "Anxiety and Depression in Young Children of Divorce." *J Clinical Child Psychology* 19, no. 1 (1990): p. 26–32.

6. Kutcher, S., and P. Marton. "Affective Disorders in First-Degree Relatives of Adolescent Onset Bipolars, Unipolars, and Normal Controls." *J Am Acad Child Adolesc Psychiatry* 30, no. 1 (1991): p. 75–78.

7. Warner, V., M. M. Weissman, L. Mufson, and P. J. Wickramaratne. "Grandparents, Parents, and Grandchildren at High Risk for Depression: A Three-Generation Study." *J Am Acad Child Adolesc Psychiatry* 38, no. 3 (March 1999): p. 289–296.

8. American Psychiatric Association. *Diagnostic and Statistical Manual of Mental Disorders*. 5th edition. 2013. doi.org/10.1176/appi.books.9780890425596.dsm04.

9. American Psychiatric Association, *Diagnostic and Statistical Manual of Mental Disorders*.

10. Lyness, Jeffrey M. "Patient Education: Depression in Adults (Beyond the Basics)." Edited by Peter P. Roy-Byrne and David Solomon. In UpToDate. https://www.uptodate.com/contents/depression-in-adults-beyond-the-basics.

11. Elevation Worship. "Won't Stop Now." Track 1 on *Hallelujah Here Below*. Elevation Worship, 2018.

12. American Psychiatric Association, *Diagnostic and Statistical Manual of Mental Disorders*.

13. Lyness, "Patient Education: Depression in Adults (Beyond the Basics)."

14. American Psychiatric Association, *Diagnostic and Statistical Manual of Mental Disorders*.

15. Lyness, "Patient Education: Depression in Adults (Beyond the Basics)."

16. Housefires. "Joy." Track 8 on *Housefires*. Housefires, 2014.

17. American Psychiatric Association, *Diagnostic and Statistical Manual of Mental Disorders*.

18. Lyness, "Patient Education: Depression in Adults (Beyond the Basics)."

19. American Psychiatric Association, *Diagnostic and Statistical Manual of Mental Disorders*.

20. Lyness, "Patient Education: Depression in Adults (Beyond the Basics)."

21. Thurlow, Jon, and Harvest. "When I Lock Eyes on You / Your Love Is Extravagant." Track 4 on *There in the Middle*. Tribl, 2020.

22. American Psychiatric Association, *Diagnostic and Statistical Manual of Mental Disorders*.

23. Lyness, "Patient Education: Depression in Adults (Beyond the Basics)."

24. García-Toro, M., E. Vicens-Pons, M. Gili, M. Roca, M. J. Serrano-Ripoll, M. Vives, A. Leiva, A. M. Yáñez, M. Bennasar-Veny, and B. Oliván-Blázquez. "Obesity, Metabolic Syndrome and Mediterranean Diet: Impact on Depression Outcome." *J Affective Disorders* 194 (2016): p. 105–108.

25. Molendijk, Marc, Patricio Molero, Felipe Ortuño Sánchez-Pedreño, Willem Van der Does, and Miguel Angel Martínez-González. "Diet Quality and Depression Risk: A Systematic Review and Dose-Response Meta-analysis of Prospective Studies." *J Affective Disorders* 226 (2018): p. 346–354.

26. Li, Ye, Lv Mei-Rong, Wei Yan-Jin, Sun Ling, Zhang Ji-Xiang, Zhang Huai-Guo, and Li Bin. "Dietary Patterns and Depression Risk: A Meta-analysis." *Psychiatry Research* 253 (2017): p. 373–382.

27. Elevation Worship, and Maverick City Music. "Jireh." Track 2 on *Old Church Basement*. Elevation Worship, 2021.

28. American Psychiatric Association, *Diagnostic and Statistical Manual of Mental Disorders*.

29. Lyness, "Patient Education: Depression in Adults (Beyond the Basics)."

30. Hillsong Young & Free. "World Outside Your Window." Track 1 on *All of My Best Friends*. Hillsong, 2020.

31. American Psychiatric Association, *Diagnostic and Statistical Manual of Mental Disorders*.

32. Lyness, "Patient Education: Depression in Adults (Beyond the Basics)."

33. Thomas D. E., E. J. Elliott, and G. A. Naughton. "Exercise for Type 2 Diabetes Mellitus." *Cochrane Database of Syst Rev*, no. 3 (July 19, 2006). doi: 10.1002/14651858.CD002968.pub2.

34. Cornelissen, V. A., and N. A. Smart. "Exercise Training for Blood Pressure: A Systematic Review and Meta-analysis." *J Am Heart Assoc* 2, no. 1 (Feb. 1, 2013). doi:10.1161/JAHA.112.004473.

35. Cooney, G. M., K. Dwan, C. A. Greig, D. A. Lawlor, J. Rimer, F. R. Waugh, M. McMurdo, and G. E. Mead. "Exercise for Depression." *Cochrane Database Syst Rev* (September 12, 2013). doi:10.1002/14651858.CD004366.pub6.

36. Harber, V. J., and J. R. Sutton. "Endorphins and Exercise." *Sports Medicine* 1, no. 2 (1984): p. 154–171.

37. Bethel Music. "This Is What You Do." Track 10 on *The Loft Sessions*. Bethel Music, 2012.

38. American Psychiatric Association, *Diagnostic and Statistical Manual of Mental Disorders*.

39. Lyness, "Patient Education: Depression in Adults (Beyond the Basics)."

40. Upper Room. "Emmanuel (Champion of the World)." Track 9 on *Land of the Living (Live)*. UPPERROOM/The Fuel Music, 2020.

41. Housefires. "The Way (New Horizon)." Track 1 on *We See Yes*. Housefires, 2017.

www.ingramcontent.com/pod-product-compliance
Lightning Source LLC
Chambersburg PA
CBHW042339150426
43195CB00006B/112